Text copyright © 2024 Noah Filipiak

All rights reserved. No part of this publication may be reproduced, stored in a retrieval system, or transmitted in any form or by any means–electronic, mechanical, photocopy, recording, or any other–except for brief quotations in printed reviews, without the prior permission of the publisher.

All Scripture quotations, unless otherwise indicated, are taken from The Holy Bible, New International Version, NIV. Copyright © 1973, 1978, 1984, 2011 by Biblica, Inc.

Cover design: Zane Ogle

NEEDED NAVIGATION

A TEEN'S GUIDE TO HIS OR HER IDENTITY IN CHRIST IN A SEX & PORN-FILLED WORLD

NOAH FILIPIAK

ACKNOWLEDGMENTS

I want to say a huge thank you to Ryan Wong and Matt Bushart for being incredible editors of this book. You made it so much better! Also tons of gratitude for Maverick, Sky, and Asher for being fantastic teen beta readers and giving great feedback. And thank you to Crystal Renaud Day for writing the foreword and for all the amazing work you're doing to help women be free from porn and unwanted sexual behavior.

CONTENTS

Foreword	ix
About this Book	xiii
1. A Teen Who Loved Jesus But Couldn't Stop Looking at Porn	1
Small Group Discussion Questions	11
2. What's the Problem with Porn?	13
Small Group Discussion Questions	23
3. God's Better Plan	25
Small Group Discussion Questions	35
4. Filling That Emptiness	37
Small Group Discussion Questions	49
5. How to Stop Looking at Porn	51
Small Group Discussion Questions	63
6. Navigating Purity Culture	65
Small Group Discussion Questions	79
Further Resources	80
Notes	83

FOREWORD

I was exposed to pornography—a hardcore, pornographic magazine—at the age of 10 years old. Home alone one afternoon after school, I was confronted by a magazine neglectfully left out on the sink in my older brother's bathroom. *And he was only 15!* That one moment—just a few pages—took me on a nearly ten-year struggle with pornography and compulsive masturbation. While most of you who picked up this book may have been exposed to porn differently (e.g. social media, gaming, websites), let me just say regardless how, the result is probably the same.

Oh, and did I mention yet that I am female?

My entire existence as a teenage girl was spent living with a secret addiction that filled me with tremendous shame. Plus, I believed I was the only one. When I was in the throes of my addiction, there were literally no resources available for women or girls facing a porn problem *(in fact it would be a decade before there would be and I was the one who wrote it!)*. It wasn't until I was nearly 20 years old that I discovered other females consumed porn, too. That was when I met another woman who shared her story with me and supported me on a path of healing. Long before then, I could only have dreamt of finding a resource like *Needed Navigation* to show me there was hope. Hope not only for freedom and wholeness, but hope also that I wasn't so debilitatingly alone.

Fast forward, I don't woulda-coulda-shoulda. Of course I wish I had never contributed to someone else's abuse *(as pornography is a form of human sex trafficking)*. However, I spent too much time living in shame to continue feeling bad about my past. Especially since God has redeemed my story again and again as I have been working professionally in the area of female pornography addiction for over fifteen years. Using my story to help other women be set free from pornography through my ministry SheRecovery has been the single greatest gift of my life.

I had the pleasure of meeting Noah Filipiak when he invited me on his show, *The Flip Side Podcast,* to discuss female pornography addiction and to share my own story. What sets Noah apart from most men in this work is his desire to bring women and teen girls into the conversation of pornography use and recovery. *That shouldn't be a rare quality!* Noah understands that pornography doesn't discriminate between male and female. God created each of us, male and female, in the image of God (Genesis 1:27) and in doing so He made both genders with sexual desire. To be sexual is to be human, and to be human is to struggle.

Noah also knows what it is like to be a teenager struggling with pornography. Like me, he has been where many of you have been. Noah found freedom from pornography... and so did I. If *we* can do it... so can *you*! But none of us can do it *alone*. I encourage you to read Noah's words with a readiness in your spirit to lean into the good work God is already doing in you and with an openness to confess and be accountable to do the next right thing in front of you. You have everything to gain, and nothing to lose *(except hopefully the porn!)*.

Let all that I am praise the Lord; may I never forget the good things he does for me. He forgives all my sins and heals all my diseases. He redeems me from death and crowns me with love and tender mercies. He fills my life with good things. My youth is renewed like the eagle's! Psalm 103:2-5 NLT

Crystal Renaud Day, MA
 CEO & Founder, Living on Purpose / SheRecovery
 www.sherecovery.com

ABOUT THIS BOOK

I wrote a book for men called *Beyond the Battle: A Man's Guide to His Identity in Christ in an Oversexualized World*.[1] The aim of *Beyond the Battle* is to help men see that what they are looking for from porn, sex, and women can only be found in the love of Jesus. The book can certainly be read by women as well, but it targets some hang-ups that are unique challenges to most men.

As I've had opportunities to speak at churches about sex and pornography, I'm often asked for a resource I'd recommend for teens. While I'm sure there are some great resources out there, I wanted to provide my own that follows the path of *Beyond the Battle*. This is a path that goes beyond surface-level solutions and gets to the root. It's a path that examines what's beneath our desires for sexual sin and how God wants us to get those desires met in healthy ways, at any stage of life.

And seeing as my struggle with pornography started when I was a teenager, and I suffered through the entirety of my teenage years without anyone talking about pornography, I feel extra motivated to write this book to you. I want to give you what I wish I had during those confusing, lonely years of isolation.

Another unique feature of this teen edition is that it is for young women as well as young men. Teen girls are looking at pornography at ever-increasing rates due to the proliferation of smartphones, popular culture's obsession with sex, and the widespread acceptance of pornography. 93% of boys and 62% of girls first see porn before they turn 18.[2] Among college-aged adults, 87% of men and 31% of women report using pornography.[3] Another study shows that 91.5% of men and 60.2% of women consume porn.[4]

When porn is talked about as a guy-only problem, it adds extra shame and unnecessary stigma onto girls and women who are struggling with it. While men and women may experience porn differently, we are all in the same boat of needing Jesus, grace, and community.

This book is not meant to be comprehensive instruction about sex for adolescents. We will specifically be looking at pornography as well as God's design for sex and how that affects you both now and in the future.

Since it's not a comprehensive book about sex, there are some really important topics it is unable to cover such as human sexuality and the LGBTQ+ spectrum, which are as relevant to teens today as they have ever been. I highly recommend Preston Sprinkle's book *Living in a Gray World: A Christian Teen's Guide to Understanding Homosexuality*[5] if you want to explore this topic further. There are also many great resources at The Center for Faith, Sexuality & Gender's website, www.centerforfaith.com.

I'm also not assuming that every teen who reads this

book is already looking at pornography. Praise God I know some of you are not, which is so awesome, and I hope this book helps keep you from it forever. I hope that it helps you be a safe person for your friends to talk to about their struggles with porn. But the statistics do show that the majority of teens, including Christian teens, are looking at porn. Or at minimum, the vast majority of teens have been exposed to porn at some point and so I am writing with that audience in mind.

In my own personal struggles with lust and porn, I define "porn" much more broadly than the statistical surveys do. I'm including sex scenes and nudity in popular TV shows and movies, as well as "edging" behaviors like lusting over images of men or women in swimsuits and underwear, which can be found almost anywhere you look on any social media channel. And let's not forget all the scantily clad internet ads and YouTube thumbnails that appear out of nowhere when you're minding your own business online.

Broadening the definition of porn is not to add extra rules to follow; it's simply identifying that the lust and fantasy cycle of fixating on these images will do similar things to our hearts and minds as hardcore porn, so it's something we need to be honest with ourselves about. We'll get to that more later in the book and I only put it here to say that this is a topic that affects all of us.

I use the word "addiction" to describe my own relationship to porn. You may or may not relate to that word and that's okay. I use it for myself to describe a behavior that I wanted to stop, but was unable to on my own strength. And though I have overcome the addiction, I still have to keep my guard up as my brain has been shaped to crave something I don't actually want. You may say, "I just like porn or am just curious about it. I'm not addicted to it." This book is still for you.

I want you to know I am proud of you for picking up this book. I know you are going through a tumultuous part of life, full of new things and excitement, but also immense insecurities and awkwardness. And I know there's a ton of pressure on you to keep up with what's considered cool by friends and teen pop culture. Sometimes you're going to get things right, and other times you're going to do things you later regret. I've been there. We've all been there. That is a part of the teenage experience and God's grace is with you both now and throughout your entire life. He loves you so much and is so pleased to call you his child.

I know you may be feeling intense guilt and shame around the subjects of sex and porn. I want to celebrate with you that Jesus' perfect sacrifice on the cross covers all the sins you and I have ever committed and ever will commit, including those in the area of sex and porn. The power of his grace can fuel your courage if you let it. Grace is more powerful than shame or guilt. Grace wins. It takes courage to read this book. It takes even more courage to read it with a friend or a trusted Christian adult. But I know you have that courage! And I know when you take that step of faith and courage, you won't regret it. In fact, I know that it will be what brings you freedom, which is the last thing Satan wants. Don't let him get his way. Keep reading! Keep being vulnerable! Invite a Christian friend or youth pastor (or even a parent!) to read this book with you.

I sincerely hope this short book can be a light in the darkness for you so you don't have to try to figure all of this stuff out on your own. I highly recommend you to read it with a group. There are discussion questions at the end of each chapter.

CHAPTER 1
A TEEN WHO LOVED JESUS BUT COULDN'T STOP LOOKING AT PORN

I grew up in the Stone Age. Dinosaurs roamed the earth and there was no internet. It's hard to imagine nowadays with smartphones and streaming channels everywhere you look, but it's true. As a kid, my brothers and I watched Saturday morning cartoons *because that was the only time they were on.* And we didn't get to pick the episode. And they had commercial breaks every few minutes. We didn't even have Nickelodeon at my house. I was a deprived child!

The world started to shift on its axis though when I was in junior high (or maybe you call it middle school… why we have two names for the same years of school is one of life's greatest mysteries). It was the mid-1990's (yes, I was born last *century!*) and the home computer, equipped with the internet, was fast becoming a common household appliance like the television or microwave. Everyone was getting one, including my parents. And this was well before the days of laptops. These behemoths sat on a desk in your living room with a tower on the floor and an enormous cube-shaped monitor hulking on the tabletop.

The stars aligned in such a way that I hit puberty at the same time the World Wide Web became available to me. This was unfortunate timing. You see, before the internet if you wanted to access pornography you had to physically walk into a store, grab the magazine or video that you wanted, and lay it on a countertop in front of an actual human being. That human being would look at you while they scanned your merchandise and you handed over your money, with some type of audible conversation happening between the two of you (and technically it was illegal to sell these items to those under the age of 18). These were all things I was never going to do, especially as a 7th or 8th grader. Of course, some boys found a family member's stash of magazines or videos and would steal them, but this still required incredible intentionality of choice to embark on and complete such a mission.

But the internet took all of those magazines and videos and put them right in my living room, just a click away, with no one watching. Instead of the unlimited barriers between 8th grade me and the adult book store (my faith in Jesus at the top of that list), the internet provided a nearly barrier-free on-ramp to the porn superhighway. I just had to wait until my parents went out to dinner or went to bed.

Please know I wasn't licking my chops to dive in to porn. But knowing an intoxicating, mysterious world of pleasure was literally sitting next to my sofa, accessible by a simple click of a mouse, eventually became too much for a 13-year-old to resist. And I didn't even start out by looking at nudity. Though no one had ever talked to me about it, as a strong Christian I knew there was something sinful about looking at naked women. I vowed I would only look at underwear and swimsuit photos and nothing beyond that. But as many of you have experienced, the brain's addictive cycle kicks in once it starts to get a dopamine hit off the stimulus of lustful images, especially when accompanied with masturbation. (Dopamine is the brain chemical that makes you feel pleasure) Just like a gateway drug, eventually the lower-level stimulus from a swimsuit photo isn't enough and your brain's appetite for the dopamine hit requires a bigger dose to get the same high. Soon swimsuit photos were in my rearview mirror and a full-blown porn addiction was on.

I want to tell you my story at the beginning of this book because I want you to know you're not alone and that to some degree, I can relate. I also want to set the foundation of grace as early as possible. Grace is the forgiveness (and love!) that Jesus shows us when we ask him to forgive us of our sins. Whenever we are talking about pornography or any other type of sexual sin, we need to be talking about grace. 1 John 1:9 tells us: *If we confess our sins, he is faithful and just and will forgive us our sins and purify us from all unrighteousness.*

Amen to that!

The best way to set an environment of grace is to be reminded that we are all in the same boat. We are all in the same boat of *needing* Jesus' grace and, praise God, he showers it on all who call on his name. We need his grace because we have sinned. This should not be a shocker to grace-believing Christians, (anyone who has experienced grace has first sinned!) but in the church we often act like it is. If you've called on his name to forgive you of your sins, then you are my sister and brother, and we are siblings-in-Christ who have been washed clean by his grace. We'll unpack that more later in Chapter 4, but for now let's just celebrate that before we go any further.

If you've never asked Jesus to forgive you of your sins, which only he can do through his death on the cross and resurrection from the dead, do so now and you too will have this grace covering you and making you whole and new.

As I share my story, it's as one who was and is forgiven by grace (and loved by God!). I'd love to see churches who say they believe in grace share more stories like this about each individual's reason for needing grace. Let's not just say we believe in grace, let's live it out. My list of needing grace is long, but a struggle with pornography and sexual sin has played a leading role.

A key piece to my story is that I loved Jesus as a teenager. I was a leader in my youth group and was sharing the gospel regularly with my friends. I wasn't living a double-life like some of my youth group friends were, putting a good face on at church, but living just like a non-Christian when it came to reveling in pornography.

I was not reveling in pornography. I was addicted to it, was deeply convicted about it, told God a million times that "this was the last time," but could never figure out how to stop.

Back in the mid-90's, nobody in my neck of the church world was talking about pornography. The internet was so new, no one had grasped its ramifications. My parents knew I loved Jesus and they had every reason to think I'd be just as likely to beat up a kid at school and steal his lunch money as I would be to start looking at internet porn. To them, and to the church world, pornography was a choice. A good Christian kid won't choose that, so we don't need to worry about it. Just like I wouldn't choose to walk into an adult bookstore to buy pornography. Which I wouldn't. But internet porn changed everything. Everything except the way the church talked about it.

I went to church or youth group three times a week (Sunday morning, Sunday night, and Wednesday night). I went to every youth camp, conference, missions trip, and retreat. I never–and I mean *never*–heard anyone talk about pornography. If they had, I wonder how different my journey could have been. If someone had reached their hand out to a Jesus-loving teen like me and said, "You don't have to do this alone, I'll help you," I know I would have taken that hand. And I believe taking that hand would have spared me from years of addiction and having to unlearn all the ways porn warped my brain.

I tried everything I could to stop. I remember putting Bible verses on index cards and posting them around my room. I would put X's on my calendar on the days I looked at porn, trying to motivate myself into a long streak of purity. I even got caught by my parents once, when I was sixteen. They had found the history on our family computer's web browser and interrogated me about it. I was crushed. I was so convicted, I thought for sure I'd never look at porn again. I remember sleeping on the floor of my room out of remorse the way David did in 2 Samuel 12:16 when the prophet Nathaniel confronted him about his adulterous affair with Bathsheba. I was that convicted. But sadly, after a week of sleeping on the floor, I figured out how to delete the computer's browser history and I was right back at it. Addiction defeated conviction.

My dad was pretty upset during that confrontation. Again, to him and I think to the vast majority of parents from the pre-internet generation, the paradigm for a kid looking at internet porn was the same as if they went out of their way to acquire it from an adult bookstore. There was not a widespread understanding about the brain science behind addiction. Nor was there any understanding about how bringing porn into our living rooms was setting up so many adolescents (and adults) with an addiction they would have never had if porn stayed behind the black curtain of the back room of the video rental store.

I remember being a kid at Blockbuster (These were entire stores where you would pay money to rent a movie on VHS tape for a few nights! Always being reminded to "Be Kind, Rewind" the tape when finished.) We would look for movies to watch as a family and I'd see a back room in the store labeled "Adult," often with a black curtain over it. There was nothing alluring or appealing about it to me.

When I got caught looking at internet porn at age sixteen, one of the first things my dad asked me was if this is what I was doing when I was over at my friends' houses. If we were huddling together to look at pornography for hours on end. I couldn't imagine doing such a thing with my friends. I didn't want to be looking at porn and I wasn't proud of it. I had fed an initial curiosity inside of me, which grew into a craving. That craving's appetite grew and grew and became out of control. It controlled me as I sought out more pornography to satisfy it, but all of that was in private.

I do remember my friends on the baseball team at my public high school openly talking about the pornographic videos they were watching. They would talk about it in the middle of practice when a coach wasn't around. I remember one guy giving recommendations on the good porn videos versus the bad ones in vivid detail, with others chiming in their thoughts about the same video titles they had seen. I am not judging you if this is or was your experience with porn. I point it out to show how an addicted Christian teen who didn't want to look at porn experienced it versus teens who had no problem with it whatsoever and talked openly about it. I think my dad thought I was in this second group, as it was the only association he, and most of the church, could conceive for pornography.

My binge-purge relationship with porn continued into college. Every time was "the last time," according to my sincere promises to God. And I always felt like garbage immediately afterward, which for me was after masturbating. The practices of porn and eventual masturbation were always intertwined for me. Once masturbation was over, my desire for the porn went away and I saw it for what it was. Sober-minded, I committed to never doing it again. Sometimes I'd last a few days, other times only a few hours.

I was never okay with my struggle, but I had no idea how to talk to anyone about it. I genuinely believed I could fix it myself, which is a lie from Satan that so many of us believe. I went to college to study to become a youth pastor, yet I was still looking at pornography in the Christian college dorms when no one else was around. This was when reality really began to hit me. How could I become a pastor with a clean conscience and have a secret porn habit behind the scenes? I knew I needed to act.

I was a freshman in college and had become friends

with Dave, a sophomore Resident Assistant in my dorm. I respected Dave's walk with the Lord and enjoyed hanging out with him. After yet another instance of promising God, "this was the last time," but knowing that it wouldn't be, I finally had to admit that I could not do this in my own power.

There's a certain level of emotional pain that comes with telling someone you're struggling with pornography. It's why we don't do it. It's uncomfortable and we don't choose to go out of our way to do painful or uncomfortable things. Change is painful, so we just stay the same. But my friend Jason likes to say, "When the pain of staying the same becomes greater than the pain of change… THAT'S when people change."

Staying the same is painful too. The garbage feeling after a porn binge is painful. The feeling like there's something getting in the way of your connection with God is painful. It's painful when you start dating someone and they ask you if you look at porn, or they don't ask but you hope they never find out. You hope no one ever finds out. It's painful when someone borrows your phone or laptop and all you can do is hope they don't stumble upon a hidden file or search history.

As you get older, things get even more painful. Maybe like me, you're studying to become a pastor or you want to be a church leader yet you can't stop looking at porn. That's painful. Maybe you think your porn habit will go away once you get married, but it doesn't, and now you've brought this untamed beast into your marriage. That's painful to hide from your spouse, and even more painful when you get found out. It's painful when porn isn't enough and you start acting out sexually in riskier ways with real people.

Somewhere along this path, there comes a point when you're tired of the pain. Going to the doctor to get a shot might be painful, and you're afraid, and that fear has kept you home this whole time. But the pain of your infection has become even worse. It's unbearable. Yes, going to the doctor will hurt. Telling someone about your porn habit will hurt. But the pain of staying the same will hurt even more.

My hope and prayer for you as you pick up this book is that you are ready for change. That you are no longer content with the status quo of managing a porn habit while trying to be faithful to God in all the other areas of your life. As an adult who grew up in the Stone Age and who has had to work hard to unlearn what porn taught me, I can say confidently that the earlier you make the choice to change, the more thankful you will be years from now.

SMALL GROUP DISCUSSION QUESTIONS

CHAPTER 1

1. What stood out to you about Noah's story?

2. Noah described the church not talking about pornography at all when he was a teenager. Has that changed in your experience and if so, in what way?

3. What have you been taught about pornography up to this point? This teaching can be formal or informal. (e.g. How do your friends talk about it? What's the perception you get about it from music, TV shows, or movies?) What have your parents or church said about it?

4. Have you ever heard another person give a testimony about struggling with and/or overcoming pornography? If so, what did you learn from it?

5. Noah said there is pain involved in seeking help for a porn habit. What type of pain was he referring to?

6. Noah also said there is pain involved in managing a porn habit and not getting help. What would be painful about that?

7. Why might a person finally choose to reach out to get help?

CHAPTER 2
WHAT'S THE PROBLEM WITH PORN?

If I grew up in the Stone Age of Fred Flintstone, you are growing up in the high-tech age of George Jetson (Does anyone even know who these old cartoons are anymore?). While we haven't figured out flying cars yet, people are talking into their watches and riding on hoverboards, just like the science fiction shows of my childhood predicted.

Today, the average age of first exposure to pornography is 12 years old.[1] The number one reason for this is because smartphones are everywhere, which is the biggest societal change by far from my teenage years to now. The hard drive tower and cube-monitor that took up half my living room is now living in your pocket. The porn that went from the adult bookstore to my dial-up desktop computer is now living inside every iPhone and Android, one easy swipe away. While I had to wait for my parents to go to bed in order to sneak into the living room (hoping to not get caught red-handed), you can access an unlimited amount of porn anytime, anywhere.

This easy access has certainly affected adults as well,

but not in the same way it does the still-developing brain of a child or adolescent. While porn gives all of us unrealistic pictures of men and women and sex, a child's brain can't distinguish between reality and what's on the screen, starting a thought pattern that is very hard to break later in life.

When my kids were really young, they'd get scared watching the most basic computer-animated movie. They understood that cartoons weren't real, but when they saw a live action film with human actors that also had talking animals or monsters, they thought these creatures must be real (and living under their beds). We were watching the PG-rated Christian movie, *The Chronicles of Narnia: The Lion, the Witch and the Wardrobe,* and my poor kids were terrified! Talking animals! Half human-half horses! Their brains weren't developed enough to distinguish reality from Hollywood fantasy and so they seriously questioned their safety in the world.

Now take this same concept and apply it to pornography and you have very young children who are being sexually abused by porn, exposed to things no young mind (and no mind, period) is ever meant to be exposed to. It's only natural for the child's mind to think this is how things are in real life, which has vast repercussions on ways kids and teens act out sexually both in their childhood and adult years.

What's really surprising to me is how so few are sounding the alarm about this. Kids are being raised on porn (while cases of rape are skyrocketing)[2] and instead of our culture seeing the problem and doing something about it, we've just normalized it. I recently ran a Facebook ad advertising the online small groups I lead for men through my book *Beyond the Battle.* It had a picture of the book and said, "Tired of Porn? Read the book. Join a group. Grow closer to Jesus." I was shocked at the comments men were posting underneath this public ad. Many mocked me, some mocked Jesus. Some tagged their porn-loving friends along with snide remarks. One comment that stood out to me was, "Grow up and go away." I can understand guys yucking it up about porn when they're privately hanging out together, but these comments were public with each man's name and face attached to it. I'm thinking, "Don't you know your mother could be reading these!?" Or a wife or girlfriend. Maybe they figured they didn't need either because they loved porn so much.

It reminded me how culturally accepted porn is today. So many people are looking at porn and, more broadly, at other sensual, lustful stimuli, that the only way to cope with such a widespread addiction is to normalize it. If everyone was addicted to heroin, it would be hard to admit that it was a problem. The only way to feel okay about things would be to celebrate heroin, and be okay with the fact that it was getting mixed in with the Fruit Loops cereal that 8-year-olds around the world were eating for breakfast.

I say all of this to emphasize grace again. I don't want to normalize the sin of lust or pornography, but we do need to normalize the conversation. If there was a pie chart representing the sins I struggled with as a teenager, it felt like pornography occupied 95% of it, yet the discipleship instruction I received only focused on the remaining 5%. This is even more magnified today with parents giving their children and teens unlimited access to lust and porn in the shape of a pocket-sized rectangle, most of the time with little to no safeguards in place. It's only a matter of time before you go looking for porn, or it comes looking for you.

Because porn has been so normalized, there's a good chance that some of you readers might be wondering what's actually wrong with it. When I do hear porn talked about by pastors, one of my biggest pet peeves is when a simple statement is made about how porn is bad or sinful, but they don't explain why. This isn't just a religious rule to follow.

My second pet peeve is if they ever do say why, they just leave it there, without giving the positive alternative or solution to porn (hint: it's not marriage, which we'll talk about in Chapter 3). And without a solution, they don't give a realistic way to stop looking at it. It's just, "Porn is bad, you should stop. Good luck."

We'll get to solutions soon, but first we need to have clarity on why porn is even a problem.

67% of teens say they feel "OK" about how much porn they watch.[3] 90% of teens are either encouraging, accepting, or neutral when they talk about porn with their friends.[4] The following list isn't meant to scare or shame you, it's meant to wake up the teens who fall into those percentage groups. And if you are a teen who already knows porn is harmful, let this list motivate you to be even more tenacious in doing all you can to find freedom from it.

After each of the following facts, ask yourself, "Do I really want this for my life?"

PORN INCREASES YOUR CHANCE OF DIVORCE

Research shows that 56% of divorce cases involved one party having an obsessive interest in pornographic websites.[5] I can testify to this personally in two ways. One is as a husband who almost got a divorce in order to pursue a promiscuous life because of the way porn warped my brain about sex. The other is as a leader of our *Beyond the Battle* men's groups,[6] with so many guys who have lost their marriages due to a porn habit they couldn't stop. Every single one of these men wishes they could go back to their teenage years, to where you are now, and get the help they needed to be free from porn. To get the help which would have spared them and their loved ones so much pain.

Research shows that when neither spouse is viewing porn, higher relational quality is reported on *every measure* of the study in comparison with marriages where an individual is viewing pornography.[7]

PORN AFFECTS YOUR MENTAL HEALTH

Studies have found a link between pornography and increased rates of depression,[8] anxiety,[9] loneliness,[10] lower life satisfaction,[11] and poorer self-esteem and overall mental health.[12]

One of the primary reasons for these devastating effects on our mental health is because porn is a lie. We crave intimacy. Porn promises intimacy, but it can't deliver. It's like being really thirsty and seeing a fridge full of water bottles and your favorite soft drinks. You rip off a cap and start chugging, only to realize after the bottle is empty that once the liquid hit your tongue, it turned into dust. Now you're even *more* thirsty! So you rip the cap of the next bottle and chug away again. And again. And again.

PORN LEADS TO HIGHER SUICIDE RATES

17% of sex addicts have attempted suicide and 72% have thought of it.[13] The 17% attempted suicide rate is nearly four times the rate for the general population of 4.6%. (While porn addiction and sex addiction sound quite different, porn addiction would fall under this larger umbrella term for clinical and research purposes.)

PORN DOES SIMILAR THINGS TO YOUR BRAIN AS HEROIN

The reason drugs like heroin are addictive is because they light up the brain's reward center, releasing a pleasure chemical called dopamine. This release happens naturally in response to behaviors we experience as positive like eating good food or getting a paycheck. It tells our brain that this is a good thing and to keep doing it. The message becomes so powerful that we become hardwired to do the thing that brings this reward. God made our brains this way, to reinforce good, rewarding behavior. But a drug like heroin hijacks this system, getting "high" off it with a cheap way to induce a dopamine rush. And you guessed it, the more you take heroin, the more heroin you need to get the same level of rush. Eventually leading to an overdose.

Does this sound familiar? It probably does if you

struggle with pornography. That's because pornography and heroin affect our brains in similar ways, creating a hijacked dopamine rush that needs more and more stimulus. Every time you turn to your drug (porn or heroin), you are increasing your craving for more. With drugs, it's higher quantities, potency, or frequency of the drug. With porn, it's quantity and frequency, but also more extreme versions of it, often leading to real-life sexual encounters that become increasingly more deviant.[14] The cycle for more never ends.

Another part of your brain is the prefrontal cortex. This is what makes you uniquely human. The prefrontal cortex is designed to put the brakes on your impulses. It's that little voice telling you that eating a third Big Mac is a bad idea because you'll probably puke, even though your reward center is crying out for more of that sesame seed bun, special sauce, and greasy beef-flavored dopamine. The prefrontal cortex wins (hopefully!) and you stop at two burgers.

But when we become addicted to a drug or to porn, the prefrontal cortex loses. When this happens over time, brain scans have shown decreased frontal brain matter.[15] It's wild to think that repetitious porn consumption is literally shrinking our brains.

The good news is that research shows our brains can heal from the damage porn or drugs have done, but it takes time and sustained effort. The sooner you're able to stop the cycle, the better off your brain is going to be. You have an incredible opportunity to do this now, as a teenager, and I hope you take full advantage of it. All of the adult men I counsel, including myself, wish we had!

PORN TRAINS US TO BE SEXUALLY ABUSIVE

Approximately 45% of teens who consumed porn did so in part to learn about sex.[16] Another study showed that 44% of boys who watched porn reported that online pornography gave them ideas about the type of sex they wanted to try.[17]

Meanwhile, at least 1 in 3 porn videos show sexual violence or aggression.[18] Another team of researchers found that a staggering 88.2% of the most popular porn scenes contained physical violence or aggression.[19]

Another study found that 95% of the targets of violence or aggression (those being beat up, etc.) appeared either neutral or to respond with pleasure.[20]

Yet survey results show that 53% of boys and 39% of girls ages 11 to 16 reported believing that pornography was a realistic depiction of sex.[21]

So porn is showing women get raped or beat up during sex and enjoy it. Then teens are watching this, thinking it's how real sex is supposed to work.

Meanwhile, 1 in 4 real life women and about 1 in 26 men have experienced completed or attempted rape. 1 in 9 men were forced to rape someone. And 1 in 3 women and about 1 in 9 men experienced sexual harassment in a public place.[22]

So if you follow this line of logic, you see that teens are looking at porn to learn about sex. They are viewing violent sex. They are then acting out this violent sex in the form of rape and sexual abuse, thinking this is what sex is.

Pornography not only physiologically deforms our brain, it deforms the way we view sex. The connection between the rampant acceptance of porn in our culture and the rampant rates of sexual abuse are crystal clear.

PORN CONTRIBUTES TO SEX TRAFFICKING

Sex trafficking is when a human is owned by another human and forced to do sexual acts with clients for pay, with the pay going to the owner. These sex slaves are typically women or children, many who have been abducted. It is the fastest growing and second largest criminal industry in the world.[23]

There are more than 4.8 million sex slaves in the world today, more than 1 million of which are children.[24]

The average age of a girl taken into sex slavery in the United States is thirteen years old.[25]

The industry makes billions of dollars a year, with an owner able to make $150,000 to $200,000 a year per child they own.[26]

One of the ways they make all this money is through the porn industry. Owners want to make as much money as they can on their "property," so when girls aren't with clients, they are posing in front of a camera, pretending to love the attention you are giving them.

Even if you are looking at porn that didn't have anyone in it posing against their will, you are still creating a demand for the product. You're still keeping the business booming and communicating to sex slave owners that there is a demand out there for their product.[27]

PORN CAUSES ERECTILE DYSFUNCTION

Numerous studies have been done that show that the combination of habitual masturbation and porn-viewing contributes to erectile dysfunction in men. And that in these cases, a man will no longer be able to get an erection with a real female sexual partner, but will be able to with more intense forms of pornography.[28]

Imagine a substance that can shrink your brain and inhibit a guy's natural ability to be aroused by a real, human woman. That's what porn is!

SMALL GROUP DISCUSSION QUESTIONS
CHAPTER 2

1. Can you remember any movies you watched as a young child where you were confused or scared about what was real and what wasn't?

2. How is porn talked about by kids at school?

3. Why do you think spouses report higher relational quality on *every measure* (every category) of marriage when both spouses are not looking at porn? (Examples of categories might be satisfaction, fun, trust, sexual intimacy, finances, raising children, etc.)

4. If you get married someday, what type of marriage do you want to have?

5. Think about the amount of people struggling with depression and other mental health issues. Now think about the amount of people looking at porn. We are not saying that if you have depression, it's from porn, but

discuss how looking at porn might cause or worsen depression.

6. Did you learn anything new in this chapter about how the human brain works in relation to addiction and pornography?

7. What are your thoughts on people taking what they see in porn and trying to live that out in real life? What are some of the consequences of attempting that?

8. What are ways you or your youth group can take a stand against sex trafficking? Do you know of any good anti-trafficking organizations you can support? If not, check out International Justice Mission, A21, and Shared Hope International.

CHAPTER 3
GOD'S BETTER PLAN

Porn is obviously outside of God's design for sex. Even if you weren't a Christian and didn't believe in the Bible, you'd have to admit that brain damage and erectile dysfunction are not how our bodies were created to operate.

But for Christians, we can dive into Scripture and see what God's design is and isn't. In the first century, a popular phrase was, "I have the right to do anything" (1 Corinthians 6:12). That sounds familiar, doesn't it? "Don't tell me what to do with my body, I can do whatever I want." Another popular phrase from Jesus' day was, "Food for the stomach and the stomach for food," (1 Corinthians 6:13) which was used sexually to mean, "When my body wants food, I give it food. When my body wants sex, I give it sex." Again, sounds very familiar! When I see a person I want to have sex with (in porn or real life), I will treat them like an object, consuming them like a Burger King Whopper. When I'm done, I'll throw away the trash and move on until I get hungry again.

What God tells us in this same chapter of the Bible is that his design for sex is *not* to "do anything" we want or to treat our sexual organs like a hungry stomach, giving them whatever they want, whenever they want it. This type of sexual behavior is selfish and turns humans into objects. But this isn't what God wants for our hearts, even during our teenage years. As you grow as a follower of Christ, he wants you to learn what love is and for your heart to mature from selfishness to selflessness. This type of love applies whether or not you get married someday. This isn't just about how we view a spouse; it's about how we view all men and women.

In response to the objectification mindset found in 1 Corinthians, Paul (the author of the book) quotes a verse from the very beginning of the Bible: *That is why a man leaves his father and mother and is united to his wife, and they become one flesh* (Genesis 2:24). When God designed sex and marriage, he designed it to be *all* of one person joining together with *all* of another person, not just their body parts. If you mix yellow Play-Doh with blue Play-Doh, what eventually happens? They turn 100% into green Play-Doh! Two become one flesh.

Prostitution was a problem in Corinth. Not just in the back alleys and dark streets like you find today, but right out in the open. They even had pagan temples where you could go to "church" to worship by having sex with temple prostitutes. This was a common and accepted practice, like porn is today. Paul's argument is that you can't become "one flesh" with a prostitute because there's no way you can give all of yourself to him or her, for life.

When the world thinks of sex, it thinks of an act

involving sexual organs that usually takes place in a bedroom. That's certainly part of the one flesh design that God has in mind, but we would all agree that humans are so much more than their body parts. What else makes someone human? The list is infinite, but it would include things like their personality, their strengths, their weaknesses, their insecurities, their mistakes, their quirks, their passions and priorities, and so on. When I got married to my wife, I made vows that said I was accepting *all* of those things about her. And she made vows to me that she was accepting *all* of those things about me. This even includes bad gas. Yes, that's right. God's one flesh design includes bad gas. Of course my wife doesn't have this issue. I might, but we all know women don't do that sort of thing. I'm just using it as a funny illustration. I promise...

I hope you laughed there (or at least rolled your eyes), but I am trying to make a point. There are things you'd never do on a first date (like bad gas!) that are going to be a natural part of married life (hate to break it to you). This is why the one flesh design doesn't have sex on a first date, or a second, or a third. Marriage is the only relationship that can support the bond of sex the way God intended. The one flesh design for sex happens in marriage because it is the place where a husband and wife have accepted *all* of the other person, with a covenant for life. That's the ultimate definition of romantic love. It's not the front you have to put up on a first date, it's the ability to take off your mask and be held and loved and accepted, for better or worse, for richer or poorer, in sickness and in health.

Marriage is a place we don't have to hide. I'm reminded of how "Adam and his wife were both naked, and they felt no shame" (Genesis 2:25). The irony is that the world's view of sex says, "You'd better keep your body hot and sexy, because that's how you'll attain love." But God says, "I already love you. And I've designed sex within marriage where your spouse is to love you for you who are as a person, today, and for all the changes of a lifetime." Of course our body parts are a good part of who we are and are a gift from God, but they are not the totality of who we are and do not define a person's value and worth. Bodies also change over a lifetime, as does a person's health. Our world's view of sex throws people in the trash and moves on to the next Whopper or Big Mac when that happens, but God's one flesh design continues to love and honor, all the days of one's life.

The world's view of sex says, "What can I get out of this person? How can they make me feel good?"

God's view of sex says, "How can I serve this person with my whole life? How can I support and care for this person and help them feel safe?"

Do you see the difference?

SONS AND DAUGHTERS

You are years away from marriage, if you ever get married at all. My point in this book is not to say you need to get married or that it is the solution to all your sexual problems. You are dealing with sex right now. Everyone is at a different place, but perhaps you are dealing with urges for sex or porn and you don't know what to do with them. Or perhaps there are others who desire to have sex with you and you are trying to figure out what to do with the

NEEDED NAVIGATION   29

conflicting emotions this brings. Or perhaps no one has the desire to have sex with you, but you wish they did so you wouldn't feel unwanted. And if you're reading this book at age 13, all of the above may change for you if you pick it up again three to four years from now.

But for anyone at any age, it's helpful to understand that sex isn't just about sex. If it was, "I have the right to do anything," would work just fine. When we start to see that sex is about a whole person, we can start seeing people as whole *right now*, which is very much God's design. Not just his design for sex, but his design for our hearts as we live in the world he created.

While the sexual act is designed to be within a one flesh marriage, the way you see other men and women is already happening. You have a daily decision to make. Will you believe and live into God's design for sex by viewing people with dignity, or will you live into the world's view of sex and see people as mere body parts for your consumption? Porn is training you to do the second of these options, while God wants to train you to do the first.

I have three daughters who are all growing up so fast. As I type this today, they are ages 12, 10, and 6. It is very easy for me to see my daughters as whole people. Someday sooner than I want to admit, there will be boys who will face the choice on if they will see my daughters with dignity and as whole people, or if they will look at them as objects, as body parts to be consumed (whether in thought or action). I know the world we live in and I know that my daughters will be objectified in the thoughts of young men more often than they will be seen as whole people. This breaks my heart. It breaks my heart because I know and love my daughters so much. I know everything that makes them fully human and every piece of that puzzle is so precious to me. It breaks my heart that there will be guys who want to take what they can get from my daughters, then throw the rest away in the garbage, like that Burger King Whopper.

But here's the truth that will transform us: God loves my daughters more than I ever could! And he knows and cares about every fully-human piece of them. And he loves me and you more than anyone ever could. And he loves the men or women that we are tempted to objectify more than anyone ever could and he knows every puzzle piece about them that makes them fully human. What he wants is for us to view men and women in the same way. This includes the men and women who are in pornography and it includes the guy or girl you are attracted to.

This isn't to say we are going to be perfect at this, nor is it to heap shame on us for the many times we'll fail to live up to this standard. But it gives us a standard. It gives us a foundation and a direction versus the alternative of just being led like a dog on a leash to wherever our "hungry stomach" may take us. My hope is that when you look at this standard, you can see God's wisdom and beauty in it. That a society full of people who value protecting, caring, and supporting is better than a society that values the selfish consumption of others.

Remember that every man or woman you see in real life or on a screen has a mother and father out there, many like myself who adore their children for all of who they are. And more importantly, has a God out there who loves them as his precious kids. Make every day a prayer to be able to see and treat men or women in the same way.

THIS WILL CONTINUE INTO YOUR MARRIAGE

One of the biggest myths believed by single Christians who are struggling with porn is that marriage will cure them. That once you can have real sex, your desire for fake sex (porn) will go away. Makes sense, right?

Wrong.

Before I go any further, please do not get married just so you can have sex. This never ends well, and it's only a continuation of the objectification mindset. Your spouse will feel used and you'll find sex isn't as utopian as you had dreamed it would be. And it may have just elevated your addiction to even more dangerous levels than when you were single.

Sadly, the church has used sex within marriage as the carrot-at-the-end-of-the-stick for single Christians, where they can finally have the awaited prize of sex. "Don't look at porn, channel those desires toward marriage," is something I've heard all too often. But marriage will not fix your porn problem; it will only make it worse. It will make it worse because you're going to have the same problem, but the stakes will be drastically higher. You will have so much more to lose.

You'll still have the same problem unless you unlearn objectification, as we are talking about in this chapter. Being taught to get married instead of looking at porn is the same as being taught to turn your spouse into an object. Instead of objectifying the body parts in porn, objectify the body parts of your spouse. In these situations, your spouse becomes a sex vending machine, there to serve your hungry stomach's every whim (and they'd better, because you did it God's way and this is your reward, so the thought pattern goes). Do you see how this is a disaster for a marriage and is far from God's design for love?

The sex you see in porn and the sex that happens in marriage are two totally different things. Even if you aren't looking at hardcore porn, the sex you are fantasizing about in your mind or with softer porn is still of a totally different substance than the sex of marriage. The sex of porn is all about your selfish desires, while the sex of marriage is all about selfless love. The sex of porn is all about consuming body parts. The sex of marriage is all about loving a whole person.

If porn-like sex is your expectation going into marriage, you will be disappointed over and over again. Your disappointment will lead to resentment toward your spouse, and perhaps toward God. Your spouse will tire quickly of being treated as an object and will feel resentment toward you. Intimacy will grow cold and the downward spiral of rejection and resentment will take over. Meanwhile, porn will still be there, like juicy hamburgers glistening for your consumption. And don't forget, sex will no longer be unfamiliar to you and it won't be long before you go looking to someone else who will temporarily meet your warped sexual expectations. I have seen this happen time and time again.

The only way to prevent this from happening is to learn to see men and women, and especially your future spouse, as a whole person. Not as a collection of body parts for your consumption. A whole son or daughter. No different than my three daughters. It's not just porn that has to go, the porn mindset has to go as well.

Scripture to read: 1 Corinthians 6:12-20

SMALL GROUP DISCUSSION QUESTIONS

CHAPTER 3

1. Do you have a younger sibling or cousin who you love? What are all the things that make them fully human?

2. Does anyone have a funny or embarrassing first date story that they can share? (Hint: ask your youth leader!)

3. What's wrong with the statement, "I have the right to do anything (sexually)"? What are negative consequences of living that out?

4. How does it feel to be used by someone? Can you think of any non-sexual examples where someone is used by someone else?

5. What are things someone can remind themselves of to help see attractive men and women as whole people who are sons and daughters of God?

6. How can you pray for the men and women in pornography and how can praying for them help decrease the temptation to view pornography?

7. Why is it flawed thinking to believe that marriage will solve someone's porn problem?

CHAPTER 4
FILLING THAT EMPTINESS

What happens if you go grocery shopping on an empty stomach? You end up filling your cart with donuts, chips, and Oreos is what happens! As a teen this might sound like heaven, but try living on donuts, chips, and Oreos for a week and let me know how you feel.

The truth is, when we are hungry, junk food looks a lot more appealing. Something similar happens with the emptiness that lives inside all of us. This emptiness doesn't crave Nacho Cheese Doritos, it craves the feeling of being valued.

Who would you rather be in this scenario: the kid who is the star of their baseball or softball team, hitting home runs with ease? Or the kid who gets picked last for gym class kickball? The all-star slugger is getting recruited by colleges and has incredible popularity in school due to their attention-getting skill set. The last-pick kickballer is physically clumsy and gets made fun of regularly, often sitting alone at lunch.

We'd all rather be the first kid. Maybe sports aren't

your thing, but you'd rather be the lead in the musical than not make it past auditions. You'd rather get an A on the test than a D or an F. And we all want friends. We want someone who accepts us. In fact, we all have an inner drive to find acceptance, and we won't stop looking for it (and doing whatever it takes) until we find it.

One of the most intoxicating ways to feel acceptance is when the cute guy or girl shows us attention. When a person we consider valuable tells us we are valuable, we experience it and believe it. You can experience this from your parents, a teacher you admire, a group of friends, or a boyfriend or girlfriend. You can also experience it from porn.

Not only can you experience the feeling of being valuable from porn, I think it's the main reason we seek it out. And I think it's the main reason we struggle so much with objectifying men and women in real life.

The men and women in porn, including the photos or videos where it's just one person posing, almost always have a look of seduction on their face. I think this is what we are truly after. We are addicted to this naked person whose face says, "I want you, I accept you, I long for you." If the naked person were spitting in our face or cussing us out in a rage, I don't think it'd be as appealing. It's not the naked body parts we're ultimately after, it's the acceptance. When the sexy person thinks we're sexy, our sense of value skyrockets.

But in porn, it's all a lie. That person doesn't care anything about you. There's no relationship and no marriage vows, so we end up emptier than when we started, except now our brain is hooked on finding that feeling again.

The same goes for real life. Do you remember God's design for sex? It's meant to be the ultimate expression of human acceptance, but can only fulfill that within the covenant vows of marriage. Sex is a very vulnerable act. You take off all your clothes and show all your blemishes to another person. Will they still accept you or will they reject you? If they accept you, that emptiness inside gets filled.

But if the covenant vows of marriage aren't there to support the sexual act, then that momentary feeling of being filled will drain out the bottom of the hole-ridden cup faster than water through a spaghetti colander. Sex is like verbally saying "I accept you," but the rest of the relationship is what shows if that statement is true or not. Sex is like writing someone a check for a million dollars, but the rest of the relationship shows if that check will cash out or not. When you turn that little piece of paper in to the bank is when you find out if the promise actually meant anything. The covenant vows of marriage–to accept all of someone for better or worse, richer or poorer, in sickness and health, till death do us part–are that bank.

I'm not saying that marriage or married sex will ultimately satisfy you; only Jesus can do that (and every marriage has its struggles to fulfill these vows all the time). But I am saying that seeking this acceptance from porn or from sex that's not backed up by marriage vows will leave you empty in the end. Love gives, but lust always takes. And lust always breeds more lust, as what we get from it is never enough.

Sex is a very potent way to get our need for acceptance met, but it's a signpost pointing to the destination that will truly fill us. It is not the destination itself. If you've ever driven to Disney World from the Midwest like I have, you know exactly what I mean. The signs with arrows pointing to Disney World tell you where you're going, but you'd never pull the van over at the sign, post photos on social media, then head back home!

The Bible uses marriage and sex in multiple places to describe God's relationship with us (Jeremiah 2:2, 20, 23-24, 33; 3:1; John 3:29; Revelation 19:7, 21:2, 9). These passages show that God is a relational God who romantically seeks after us. He wants you and desires you. He accepts you. God longs for an intimacy with us that only married sex can symbolize. Sex is a symbol and signpost of a greater need for intimacy that we all carry with us.

So if you have a desire to look at porn, I want you to slow down and look at why. Certainly there is the surface-level physical and mental feeling that comes along with it and there's a component of natural attraction (that's been hijacked). Part of this feeling and attraction is designed by God. But I don't think that's the truest reason why we get so hooked on porn and sex. Let's go back to a point I made earlier: if a valuable person tells me I'm valuable, then I feel like I am. So perhaps the 10-out-of-10 cute guy or girl at school isn't telling you you're valuable, but you can find a photo or video of a 10-out-of-10 man or woman in pornography. Through the seductive way they're posing and acting, in combination with your mind's ability to create fantasy, you are putting yourself into this sex scene with them. And in this scene, that seductive look is for you. That look of acceptance is for you. They are telling you, "I want you, I desire you, you are valuable." This is the message that drives almost all of human behavior and is the message we want to hear above all others in life.

But just as water drains through a spaghetti colander, the feeling doesn't last. The dopamine rush passes and you're back to reality, just as empty as ever.

But if we are able to name the deeper need we are trying to meet, we can begin to find freedom from the hold that porn and sex has over us. When we can identify that these body parts are symbols and signposts, not the ultimate destination, what can we begin to do? We can see them as the symbols they are, removing the power they have over us, and we can pursue the ultimate destination instead!

Like I said before, you may not care now if your shopping cart if full of Oreos, donuts, and chips, but you will someday as an adult (or I hope you will!). There are all kinds of health problems that will catch up to you if your main four food groups are cookies, soda, chips, and donuts, not to mention some of that bad gas you sure don't want to let loose on a first date! If you're trying to minimize your junk food intake, the solution is to develop an appetite for the good stuff. If you are filled up with three helpings of Thanksgiving dinner, your craving for junk food is going to change dramatically.

Humans are created with a God-given need and drive for acceptance and validation. But *God* is the only one who can ultimately meet that need in us. This is done specifically through Jesus Christ, who is God-in-the-flesh, and who died on the cross to forgive us of our sins. God loves us so much that he put on human flesh and came to us in order to show us that love (John 1:14; Philippians 2:6-8). He pursued us and he continues to pursue us. He is pursuing you and loves you and accepts you with a love you will never find anywhere else.

If you've never believed in this love and accepted it into your life, do so now. But I imagine there are a lot of Christians reading this book who would say they already believe this, and are wondering why it's not filling up this empty space more or why they still have a desire to get this need met through pornography.

God wants us to believe in his love and forgiveness with our minds, but he also wants us to experience it. Do you remember in Chapter 2 how the brain can physically change back to its healthy, natural form after being deformed by addiction and trauma? One of the ways this can happen is through experiencing the embodied love of Jesus through other people.[1]

When we look to porn or sex to find our value, our operating system is running on the belief that we are not valuable. If I was valuable already, why would I need to go to porn or a man or woman to make me valuable? A $100 bill doesn't need a stamp of approval on it from you before you can spend it because it already has the only stamp of authority in needs from the U.S. Government. But our operating system has believed the lie that we don't have value, thus we must get this stamp–in this case from attractive men and women.

It's really important that we meditate on Scriptures like:

John 3:16,
For God so loved the world that he gave his one and only Son, that whoever believes in him shall not perish but have eternal life.

Matthew 3:16-17,

As soon as Jesus was baptized, he went up out of the water. At that moment heaven was opened, and he saw the Spirit of God descending like a dove and alighting on him. And a voice from heaven said, "This is my Son, whom I love; with him I am well pleased."

Romans 8:15-17,

The Spirit you received does not make you slaves, so that you live in fear again; rather, the Spirit you received brought about your adoption to sonship. And by him we cry, "Abba, Father." The Spirit himself testifies with our spirit that we are God's children. Now if we are children, then we are heirs—heirs of God and co-heirs with Christ

(Romans 8:15-17 makes everything the Father says to Jesus in Matthew 3:17 also true of each of us!)

and Colossians 1:22,

But now he has reconciled you by Christ's physical body through death to present you holy in his sight, without blemish and free from accusation—

In these Scriptures, you find the truth that you are already accepted! You have his stamp of approval and his stamp is the only one with authority behind it. You are accepted by Jesus so fully that when God looks at you, all he sees is blameless perfection. That's how valuable you are! You are God's precious child, his son or daughter that he holds close. When you go to God in prayer, I want you to hear God saying this message to you over and over again: *My child, I love you. I accept you. I approve of you. You are so valuable to me. I love you. I accept you. I approve of you. You are so valuable to me.*

And he does! All because of Jesus' finished work on your behalf.

We can experience this truth in prayer and we can experience it in reading the Bible and from books like this one. We can also experience it in sermons, in worship as we sing about it, or when we take the Lord's Supper at church. All of these are great ways to be reminded of the truth of our value and acceptance.

But brain science research shows that what really accelerates the healing process, meaning we actually start to believe this truth at the deepest level, is when brothers and sisters in Christ look us in the eye, speaking and embodying these truths to us.

If one of your parents have told you your whole life (directly or indirectly) that you are worthless or you don't measure up or you need to do XYZ in order to prove your value, it's only a matter of time before you start believing this is true. That you aren't valuable and you need something else to make you valuable. Teachers and coaches can communicate the same thing, as can the popular crowd, or the guy or girl you wish would date you. When we get rejected by any of the above, it reinforces the message that we are unwanted.

I meet weekly on Zoom with my *Beyond the Battle* men's group.[2] We read Scripture together that reminds us we are accepted and loved by God. We then break into smaller groups and each guy shares how his week went. Following that, the next guy speaks this truth over the man who just shared:

(Insert first name), you are our Father's son, and he loves you so much. He is so pleased with you. Nothing can add or subtract to how much he loves you and approves of you right now.

Sexual sin makes you feel like you aren't worthy of God's love, but Jesus' grace covers our sexual sin! Colossians 1:22 is true, even when it comes to sexual sin: *holy in his sight, without blemish and free from accusation.* Amen and amen and amen!

But we've heard *a lot* of messages that we don't measure up. This made a crater inside of us, compelling us to look to porn and sex to tell us that we do measure up. We need to hear over and over again from real humans that we already measure up. That we are already valuable. That we are approved and accepted, just as we are. We don't need to earn it. And eventually as we experience this message, our deepest self starts to believe it.

This is not a self-esteem or self-help positive thinking exercise; this is grounded in the rock-solid foundation of the gospel of Jesus. This is the priceless gift that the gospel of Jesus gives us.

THE FREEING GIFT OF GRATITUDE

Can you start to feel how immense God's love is for you? And how this love gives you acceptance and value? Do you see how this love and acceptance can be the Thanksgiving feast the emptiness inside of you is craving?

It's an amazing feeling when we experience these things with Jesus. There's no better foundation to build a life upon. But bad circumstances can clog up the pipes that bring this peace-filled love into our lives.

When things are flowing smoothly, we live in gratitude for how much Jesus loves us. We savor how much God approves of us and how much value we have in his sight as his precious child.

But then we get rejected by the guy or girl we have feelings for. This jars us back to feeling unwanted. "This person doesn't desire me; therefore I lack worth and value," we think to ourselves. What now happens when we go to God in prayer?

Instead of thanking him for his love and forgiveness and reflecting on how all my needs are met as his beloved child, instead of thanking him for what he *has* given me, my prayer focuses on what he has *not* given me. Now it's fine and even biblical to bring our requests to God, but we get in trouble when the heart of our prayer goes something like this, "God, give me this thing/person I want, or else…"

That "or else" could be any number of things, most of which we aren't consciously choosing, but our deeper desires gravitate toward. It could be "or else I'll go look at porn," or "or else I'll stop believing in you," or "or else I'll keep believing the lie that this guy or girl will make me whole (valuable, accepted, approved)."

But at the end of the day, our posture toward God has changed from one of gratitude (thank you for all you've given me) to entitlement (you haven't given me enough). When this happens, we have to go back to remembering the truths of the gospel. The first is that we don't deserve it. When I get caught up in my entitlement, I find myself praying to God, "Give me what I deserve." God answers me and says, "You don't want me to give you want you deserve. You deserve to be punished eternally for your sins, but I haven't given you that. I have given you my mercy instead."

Do you see how this flips a switch? My prayer has now changed from, "God, give me what I deserve; why are you holding out on me? Don't you love me? Or is there something wrong with me that you won't help me?" to "God, thank you for your mercy! Thank you that you don't give me what I deserve, which is eternal separation from you. Thank you that you give me your love instead. Thank you that you accept me and approve of me and you see me as so valuable in your sight." I can still feel the ache of whatever my bad circumstance is, but I'm not letting it be my foundation. I'm not looking to it to fill the crater inside of me. I'm going back to the gospel to be reminded that that crater is already filled, that I'm already approved and don't need a guy or girl to fill me. Your circumstance may not change. That guy or girl may never desire you romantically, but when you already know where your identity and value come from, you can mourn this loss without it shattering your faith in God or making you dive into porn to get a brief whiff of validation.

When you feel like what you have isn't enough, go to God and thank him for not giving you what you actually deserve! And thank him for the riches of his grace, love, and mercy he's given you instead.

SMALL GROUP DISCUSSION QUESTIONS

CHAPTER 4

1. What are your favorite junk foods? How would you feel if that was all you ate for a month?

2. What are different ways people try to feel valuable or accepted?

3. What are some things that can happen to a person to make them feel rejected or like they don't have value?

4. How does it make you feel that God is pursuing you, desires you, loves you, accepts you, and approves of you? What is uniquely powerful about God feeling this way about us in comparison to how any human feels about us?

5. What are some practical, regular ways you can be reminded of the truth of God's love and approval of you?

6. How does your heart feel different when you go God saying, "You haven't given me enough, you are holding out on me," versus, "Thank you so much for everything

you've given me. Thank you for giving me love, mercy, and grace that I don't deserve."

7. Do you have Christians in your life who regularly remind you (with their words and actions) that you are loved by them and God? If not, how can you increase and invest in more of these relationships?

CHAPTER 5
HOW TO STOP LOOKING AT PORN

When it comes to learning how to stop looking at porn, I see it like taking out a tree. A tree has roots and branches, and in our case, it's important to address both.

Up to this point in the book, we've been discussing root issues. I think these are the most important. If you only cut off the branches (the behaviors or symptoms) and leave the root intact, those root desires will just keep fueling new branches to grow. Kill the root, kill the tree.

But the branches are still there and need to be dealt with. It's really hard to change your heart toward porn if you keep looking at it. It's like trying to get a fire to go out; every time you look at porn, you've just added a new log to the fire.

Now that we've established the root of the problem and how to change that root, I want to get really practical about changing our behavior–the branches. But before I go any further, I want you to ask yourself, "Am I a person who wants to stop (or never start) looking at porn?" I think I've given you a lot of good reasons to stop, but only you can make this decision for yourself.

And if you say 'yes,' I want to challenge you to really show it. If someone says they want to lose weight or get in shape, what will show if they really wanted this or not? They will go to the gym. They will be active. They will eat healthier. They may even join a team or hire a trainer to hold them accountable to the things they say they want, knowing there will be days they want to give up in their own strength.

I don't want you to just say 'yes,' I want you to show your 'yes' through action.

ACTION STEPS

A game changer to stop looking at porn is to effectively use Covenant Eyes and Accountable2You on all of your online devices. These are accountability software that send email reports of all of your online activity to trusted accountability partners. They are life-changing (and life-saving) products and I use them both in tandem.

Now I know as a Christian teen that some of your parents have already tried using this software with you and you either loathe it or you've found ways around it. The first thing that needs to happen in this process is you, as a follower of Jesus, need to get on board with wanting freedom from porn. Your parents can try to protect you from it, I can try to warn you about it, but you have to be mature in your faith and make the choice that you're willing to take action steps against it. And to know that it will require some sacrifices. These small sacrifices are worth it in comparison to the rampant destruction porn will bring into your life, but you have to decide which you want more. And you have to decide you can't quit in your own strength and willpower.

I want to remind you of the countless adults I counsel away from porn and sex addictions. Many of these adults' marriages and lives have been devastated, inflicting intense pain on them and those they love the most. Every single one of them (including myself) wishes they could go back to being a teenager and stop the addiction before it grew worse. They wish they could have gotten the help they needed when they were still a teen. *You* have the opportunity that these adults would pay millions of dollars to have if they could hop in a time machine. Please take full advantage of it. This includes using online accountability software.

I had a parent say to me once, "If I tried adding this software onto my son's phone, he would ask why I didn't trust him."

This is not about if you can be trusted on the internet or not. The internet cannot be trusted! Period. Satan is using the internet to prey on our natural attractions and desires. He is hijacking and abusing them. This is not about if your parents can trust you, or even if you can trust yourself. Imagine a minefield. If a military general told a soldier, "Don't go in that field, there are mines in it," should the soldier respond and say, "What gives? I can't believe you don't trust me to not step on a mine." This isn't about trust, it's about highly destructive explosives that are scattered everywhere. There are some minefields we can and should avoid altogether and others we can learn to navigate after marking off the sections where we know the explosives are.

Another component of the parent-to-teen dynamic is we have to get past the awkwardness of talking about sex. Sex is everywhere and we need to talk about it. And we need to get past this us-versus-them mentality that can generate between parents and teens. Parents, you are not hunting your teens down, ready to punish them if you discover they're looking at porn. And teens, take the lead and talk to your parents about pornography. I know this is a huge risk and that some of you are going to have supportive parents and others won't. If you don't think your parents will be supportive, talk to your youth pastor or church youth leader. Christian adults today know how pornography is everywhere and most want to help.

If you're a parent reading this and your teen won't talk to you about porn or they don't care that they're looking at it, you still need to try, even if it's awkward. Even if they resist you now, when they are adults, I believe your son or daughter will look back at these years and be thankful they had a parent who was brave enough to care rather than someone who pretended like this wasn't an issue. Parents, approach your teen with grace and empathy, pray diligently for them, and leave the rest in God's hands.

But this is a book written to teens. So I want you teens to know that many of you have parents who want to help, but don't know how. If and when they try talking to you or helping you, welcome it. Don't wait for them to bring up adding Covenant Eyes and Accountable2You to your devices. You initiate it. Tell them you want to obey Jesus and you don't want this stuff in your life, but you know it's everywhere out there. Admit to yourself that you can't do this alone and you don't want to do it alone. I'm not saying your parent needs to be your accountability partner, but they can be a support to you.

If you are tenacious in wanting to look at porn, yes, you will find ways around software. But if you are tenacious in wanting freedom from porn, you can lock down your software so that when temptation comes, it doesn't have a way in. Remember the fire metaphor. The fire will dwindle if new logs aren't added to it. Your desires and your view of sex and men/women will change if you stop getting exposed to porn. But if you keep adding logs to the fire, that flame will burn brighter and that mindset of objectification will never change.

I use both Covenant Eyes and Accountable2You on all my devices. They do different things and I like the double coverage they provide me. I'm going to briefly explain what each one does and then provide you with promo codes to get your first 30 days free with each product. Before I begin, I want to remind us of something Jesus said:

If your right eye causes you to stumble, gouge it out and throw it away. It is better for you to lose one part of your body than for your whole body to be thrown into hell. And if your right hand causes you to stumble, cut it off and throw it away. It is better for you to lose one part of your body than for your whole body to go into hell. (Matthew 5:29-30)

Jesus wasn't saying to literally cut off your hand or gouge out your eye, but he was saying we will have to make sacrifices to attain freedom from sexual sin, and those sacrifices are worth it to those who truly want this freedom. His extreme examples are meant to wake us up to how important this is. What I'm about to prescribe to you will require some sacrifices on how you use your electronic devices, but I promise you it won't be as severe as the examples Jesus used!

Covenant Eyes monitors the images on your computer, phone, and tablet screens. It has an algorithm that detects nudity or potentially explicit images and it flags them. It then puts these images into an email that is sent to your accountability partners. The images in the email are blurred out so as to not cause the recipient to be tempted, but shows enough that they get the idea of what you were looking at. It also includes the website where the image was found. You can add an optional filter that will block some explicit sites and has a customization setting where you can add sites you uniquely struggle with to a custom block list.

Accountable2You is based on text and monitors the words you type into your devices and the words that appear on your screen. It will send accountability emails of the sites you visited and the searches you made. It will also send text messages in real time to your accountability partners if you are accessing explicit material. The double coverage of A2U for what you type in and Covenant Eyes for the images on your screen is a nice combo to seal up some loopholes you may or may not find when using only one of the programs. Another plus of using both is that A2U works on Chromebooks and Kindle Fires, while Covenant Eyes does not.

Ok, now get ready for the sacrifice, especially if you are an Apple user. Covenant Eyes and A2U work great on both Mac and PC computers. They monitor everything on your screen, regardless of what program you are using. They work equally great on Android phones and tablets. They monitor everything on your screen, all apps included. This is a great thing, as we want to be fully covered. The snag is Apple's iOS (iPhones and iPads) does not allow Covenant Eyes or A2U to monitor everything on the screen, which is a major problem. They can only monitor what's happening inside the Safari browser. This means the user can still access undetected explicit images in any app they want, from YouTube to Instagram to TikTok. For those really serious about finding freedom from porn and sexual sin, this just isn't good enough. As I mentioned at the very beginning of the book, it doesn't have to be hardcore pornography to fall under the definition of porn, and these "softer" versions are doing similar damage to your heart, mind, addictive patterns, and the ways you view men and women.

There are two solutions to this iPhone and iPad shortcoming:

The first one is to have a parent, friend, or youth leader (someone you see regularly) setup the Screen Time passcode on your iOS device and disable the ability to use the AppStore. Next, delete all apps that will give you access to explicit material. Then instead of using Instagram on the app, you go to www.instagram.com on Safari and you use it from there. Same for www.youtube.com, www.facebook.com, etc. You use the social media platforms on the browser, not the apps. These browser user experiences are not as good as the app and they won't do everything the app does. That is a sacrifice you are making (cutting off the hand and gouging out the eye) for your freedom from sexual sin and to obey Jesus. It is worth it, I promise you.

And hey, you still get to use these platforms and interact with your friends.

You can reach out to Covenant Eyes or Accountable2You customer support for more help in locking down your iPhone and iPad.

If all of this seems like too big of a hassle or if you need the features that a social media app has over the browser experience, the other option to solve the limitations of iOS is to switch to Android (gasp, I know). Now hear me out, Apple users. I readily admit that iPhones are better than Androids. And I know how well iOS devices integrate with Macs. But I'd much rather use an Android than get rid of my phone altogether, a la Jesus' hand-cutting and eye-gouging. And at the end of the day, I don't want to look at porn! Do you?

I can't tell you the number of people I've talked to who would rather have full use of their iPhone or Apple Watch than make the above changes. And no matter how much they tell me they don't want to look at porn, guess what? They do want to look at it. Because if they didn't, they'd either delete their apps and have a friend disable their AppStore or they'd switch to Android. That is what someone does who truly doesn't want to look at porn.

To download Covenant Eyes, go to www.covenanteyes.com and use promo code BEYOND to get your first 30 days free. Then install the app on unlimited devices. (For the promo code to work, you have to sign up via the website and not the app.)

To download Accountable2You and get your first 30 days free, type a2u.app/beyond or https://a2u.app/beyond into your internet browser. Do not use *www.* or the link won't work. Once you've signed up, you can download A2U onto your devices (up to 6 devices for the Personal Plan, up to 20 for the Family Plan as of this writing).

(The longer this book is in print, the more likely something in the tech world can change. If any of the above links don't work for you, visit www.noahfilipiak.com/software for up-to-date download instructions.)

This software will cost you money once the free trial is over. Talk to your parents and see if they'll cover this cost for you. Or start a bank account so you can cover it for yourself with a debit card. Talk to your youth pastor if you don't have these options. Covering the cost is another necessary sacrifice to find freedom from porn and to obey Jesus' command. The cost is a sacrifice, but it's worth it. And it's a much smaller sacrifice than losing a hand or an eye!

(I encourage you to sign up for your own account. But if you can't afford it and if you know someone who already uses Covenant Eyes, they can add you to their account as a new, separate user for free.)

LEARNING FROM RATS

The more isolated you are, the more you are going to want to look at porn. This is because God created you for connection. The less the amount of healthy connection you have in your life, the more appealing the fake connection of porn will be to you. And the greater the amount of healthy connection in your life, the more your appetite for porn's fake connection will dissipate.

As we've discussed, porn gives a temporary, fake feeling of being accepted and valued. Part of the way this works is by numbing us out to try to make our brain feel happy. But porn isn't the only vice facing teens for numbing out and tricking the brain into feeling momentary happy.

I volunteer at a local non-profit where teens hang out. I knew there was no school this particular day and I asked one of the teens what he did with his free time. He said he watched YouTube all day. My first thought was, "You watched YouTube *all day*, like 8 hours all day? How sad." He smelled like marijuana so I knew he had also been getting high while watching YouTube. This is the opposite of living. In John 10:10, Jesus says, *The thief comes only to steal and kill and destroy; I have come that they may have life, and have it to the full.* A teenage boy sitting home alone all day while numbing out to pot and YouTube is the work of the thief, stealing and destroying an entire day that could have been spent doing productive and fulfilling things. I didn't pry, but I'd bet this teen boy wasn't just watching YouTube as he sat alone all day, but also lots of porn.

I'm not judging him, and I'm not judging you if this is how you have spent entire days off. I understand the pain in this young man's life and how he is simply trying to get the pain to momentarily go away. And I understand the pathways his brain has built that tell him to go to these behaviors to solve his problem of loneliness and disconnection.

But isolation will never solve our connection problems! What a trick from Satan, the thief.

Psychologist Bruce Alexander did an experiment in the 1970's that has come to be called "Rat Park." Some rats were put in individual cages, isolated. They were offered two water bottles: one was filled with plain water and the other with heroin or cocaine-laced water. The rats would repeatedly drink from the drug-laced water bottles until they overdosed and died. (Anyone who has seen the movie *Ratatouille* should be very sad about this!)

Dr. Alexander wondered if this behavior was about the drug or if it was about the setting the rats were in. To test this, he puts rats in "rat parks," where they were free to roam and play, to socialize, and to find a mate. *And* they were given access to the same drug-laced bottles. When living in the rat park, they remarkably preferred the plain water.[1]

Do you see the profound implication of this experiment on any type of addiction? Yes, willpower is important. But creating healthy connection is even more important. If we are getting our needs met in healthy ways, we lose the necessity of getting them met in destructive ways.

This means that a teenager who is active in their church youth group, active in school sports, music groups, other extracurricular activities, has a job, has hobbies, and is intentional about hanging out with a friend group that encourages Christ-like choices is going to have much less time, energy, and need to find connection from pornography because they are already so well-connected!

Whereas a teen who scrolls TikTok and YouTube shorts endlessly, plays copious amounts of video games, and holes up in their room whenever they can is going to be an easy target for the connection-trap of pornography.

I'm not saying being busy will cure your desire for porn, but I can promise you that isolation will almost always heap on more porn.

An active lifestyle full of connection in combination

with effectively using Covenant Eyes and Accountable2You will go a long way to living a porn free life. Add in a regular community of Christ-followers who can hold each other accountable and remind each other of the root-level truths found in this book, and you have a winning combination.

SMALL GROUP DISCUSSION QUESTIONS
CHAPTER 5

1. Why is it important to take out both the "root" and the "branches" of a porn problem?

2. What are your hobbies? What is one new healthy hobby or activity you can start? (Bonus if it's something that gets you interacting in person with others)

3. If someone says they want to give up a bad habit or addiction, what are some action steps they would take that would show they really mean this?

4. Why do you think Jesus uses such extreme examples in Matthew 5:29-30 when talking about necessary sacrifices we need to make to be free from sexual sin?

5. How is your relationship with your parents around the topic of online pornography? What would happen if you asked for their help in installing Accountable2You and Covenant Eyes?

6. If you can't get your parents to help you, or you just can't bring yourself to talk to them about it, who are some other people in your life you trust and respect who can help you?

7. Why is it our natural tendency to think we can stop a bad habit or addiction all by ourselves?

8. Why do you think the rats living in "Rat Park" chose to drink the plain water instead of the drug-laced water? And why do you think the rats living alone overdosed until they died?

9. What are some ways you can fill your life with more healthy connection and community?

CHAPTER 6
NAVIGATING PURITY CULTURE

When I was growing up as a teen in the thick of what is now known as "Purity Culture," a common teaching was that you shouldn't even kiss someone until your wedding day. This was in combination with a teaching that dating itself was wrong and that romantic interaction between teen girls and guys should only take place within "courtship." Courtship happened before engagement and its primary purpose was marriage preparation. To my youth pastor's credit, he didn't teach either one of these things, but I had plenty of friends in high school and college who had read the popular books and had committed to the tenants. In fact, a girl I liked turn me down because she said she was reading a book called *I Kissed Dating Goodbye*[1], therefore she couldn't date me! (And yes, I wonder to this day if she was actually reading the book or just needed a convenient way to let me down lightly!)

These approaches may have worked for some, but a generation later we see they did large scale damage–damage that is being written about more and more by Gen

X and Millennial authors today. What I want us to look at as it applies to this book is why Christian leaders of that era (and many still today) taught the most extreme prohibitions they could for teens when it came to anything sexual or romantic.

It's been standard, biblical teaching for a long time that sex is meant for marriage alone. Prior to the sexual revolution of the 1960's, mainstream culture was also built around that value. But as sex before marriage became more normal outside of the church (and as fewer and fewer people went to church), church leaders had to double down.

One glaring problem of the Purity Culture movement was that the sin of sex before marriage became elevated above all other sins. Piles of shame were heaped onto anyone who had sex before marriage, as if they were permanently tarnished for their future spouse and somehow out of the reach of Jesus' grace.

So to avoid the worst-sin-in-the-world, it became important for Christian leaders to keep teens ten steps away from it. And since dating led to holding hands which led to kissing which led to making out which led to touching which led to sex, it was really important to keep teens from dating.

Afraid of sinning as a teen, I remember reading any article I could on, "How far is too far?" This question spurred the logic behind not kissing until your wedding day because you couldn't risk going down that slippery slope. "How far is too far" was to be as far away as possible!

Now, the Bible does teach us that God's ideal is for sex to be saved for marriage, and that sex before marriage is a sin, but in case anyone missed sex-ed class, kissing is not sex!

One of the many problems with this line of thought is you villainize your own body and the body of the person you're dating. I know of a lot of marriages where one spouse has a low sex drive or negative views about sex because Purity Culture taught them to stay away from all physical contact and to repress all desire for it. They thought they could flip the switch once they got married, but their body was preconditioned otherwise.

This leaves the other spouse feeling rejected or like their sex drive is evil and dirty. We know this isn't part of God's design for the gift of married sex, which indicates we've done something wrong in how we teach teens and singles about it in the church.

Are there risks to experiencing levels of physical contact with the opposite sex as a teen? Yes. But there are also equal, and perhaps greater, long-term risks when physical contact is deemed as evil and to be avoided at all costs.

Many of these marriages with a low libido spouse end up in divorce and/or adultery, or the marriage vows are upheld but with a lot of pain and frustration. There are Christian counselors and therapists who specialize in helping these low libido spouses go back and unlearn what Purity Culture taught them about sex during their teenage years so they can take steps toward enjoying sexual intimacy in their marriage the way God intended.

I'm not laying down any laws and not trying to answer the "How far is too far?" question for you. One of the major problems of Purity Culture was the one-size-fits-all laws and answers that were laid down for an entire generation of Christians. As if individual Christians didn't have the Holy Spirit living inside of them, whose job is to convict, lead, guide, and answer prayer. When it comes to the gray areas of singleness in modern society, I am very comfortable leaving that job to the Holy Spirit!

To navigate all this, we will have to keep several things in tension. One is that God created sex and he created penises and testicles and breasts and vaginas and clitorises and orgasms. These are not dirty words. These are all his design and are good. I want everyone taking that understanding into their marriage. It doesn't mean you need to have extensive experience with them, but it does mean you need a positive outlook on them as God-created gifts.

Another piece of this tension is that sex is meant for marriage, as we discussed in Chapter 3. But people got married much younger in the first century when the New Testament was written (as young as age 12![2]). Now there is a long gap between puberty and marriage, for those who even get married someday. This leaves a lot of room for discernment from the Holy Spirit on the best way to save sex until marriage without falling into the traps of Purity Culture.

This also leaves a lot of room for error on the pendulum of too much physical experience before marriage, or too little. But error is part of the human experience, is one of the best teachers, and is the reason we need Jesus' grace in the first place. Grace isn't an excuse to sin, but it is there to catch us as we stumble along, trying our best to figure things out.

I don't think rules will help us here, but guiding principles can.

One great guiding principle in all of these tensions is to

commit that we will not objectify or willingly let ourselves be objectified, also discussed in Chapter 3. Here's a concrete example: we've said it's not wrong to kiss before marriage. But if you are kissing someone, is it out of selfish objectification? Do you just want what this person can give you physically? Are you just kissing because it feels good? A "yes" to these questions is the same as a porn-mindset. We need to get away from that mindset.

Other relevant questions: Are you even in a committed relationship with this person that requires you to support and care for them in all aspects of their life? How old are you and what level of intimacy is appropriate for the level of commitment that your relationship is able to have?

Some authors who were raised in Purity Culture have left their faith, or are pretty close to being fully gone. You will often hear the baby thrown out with the bathwater from these authors. They chronicle the legitimate perils of Purity Culture, then conclude that sex is fine outside of marriage and that there shouldn't be any prohibitions on sex at all, including the use of pornography. We've already talked at length about why this isn't God's design and is a path that will just lead you to a different type of pain and brokenness than Purity Culture would. "I have the right to do anything," is not the solution and never has been.

MASTURBATION

The primary reason I want to include a section on masturbation in this book is because it is usually a big source of confusion for Christian teens and is something very few want to talk about. And when we don't talk about something, we just get used to hiding, which increases shame and makes us less vulnerable.

When I published my book *Beyond the Battle: A man's guide to his identity in Christ in an oversexualized world*, I also wrote a blog post titled "Is Masturbation a Sin?" that I referenced in the book. You can find that blog article here: www.noahfilipiak.com/is-masturbation-a-sin

I'll summarize some thoughts from the article here, plus say some specific things to teens.

There are many different opinions on masturbation within biblically conservative Christianity. I won't list them all here, but check out the blog article to learn more. You'll probably be surprised! In the circles I grew up in and often still swim in, the prevailing vibe is that all masturbation is sin all the time. Off the bat, I want to say I respect this view and I know it's coming from a good place. If a pastor or parent is reading this, know that I think this is a good goal and I am not here to convince you or your teens of a different view. If any reader, teen or adult, feels convicted about masturbation and you're attempting to eliminate it from your life, I fully support you in that. I'll try to write some things below that will help you.

But I do feel called to give a more biblically comprehensive answer to this question and raise caution about the various views of masturbation that are out there. I think we all need to hold our views of masturbation humbly, as it's a subject the Bible doesn't specifically mention. And we need to hold our views honestly, candidly being able to see the strengths and weaknesses of various views and how our view might harm someone, especially if it's proposed as the dogmatic from-the-mouth-of-God view. And much like Purity Culture, we need to trust the Holy Spirit to do his work in this gray area and not try to be the Holy Spirit ourselves by saying things the Bible doesn't say.

My blog article explains this in detail, but the Bible does not say masturbation is a sin. It does say lust is a sin. And while masturbation is most often partnered with lust, these are still two separate things, and it's important that we treat them as such. This is especially true when talking to young teenagers who are just going through puberty.

I realize young teens are reading this book and I'm not trying to gross you out, I promise! And I apologize in advance for grossing you out because it's probably bound to happen.

As a child's body changes into an adolescent body (a.k.a. a teen body), one of the key changes that happens is the body becoming sexually mature. A guy can get an erection and can get a girl pregnant. A girl begins ovulating and can get pregnant. These are natural, biological phenomena and shouldn't be depicted as gross or sinful by Christians. Nor should they be treated with shame. Growing into a sexually mature adult is as natural as getting taller or sprouting underarm hair. Along with these bodily changes comes the ability for young men and women to orgasm. There's nothing harmful or even necessarily sexual (you can orgasm separate from any thoughts about sex) about an adolescent discovering they can orgasm or feel pleasure in their sexual organs. This is exactly how God designed our bodies to work.

If we believe there is something shameful about this, we perpetuate Purity Culture stigmas. These stigmas deny that God made our sexual organs, orgasms, and our human bodies as part of his loving creation. These stigmas also create the negative bodily responses to sexual stimuli that can train us into deep shame over something that is completely biological. As previously mentioned, this stigma can then be carried into marriage and severely inhibit the ability to be open and available sexually to a spouse, causing catastrophic emotional damage to both spouses.

There is nothing wrong with the discovery of masturbation by an adolescent. It is natural. There are a lot of teens who have masturbated, and there are a lot of teens who haven't. You're in good company either way. I know of adult guys who have never masturbated in their entire lives. I think this is fantastic. If you've never masturbated, please don't feel like you need to start. And if you end up stumbling upon it, I don't think that's the end of the world either. Some statistics can be helpful here.

The National Survey of Sexual Health and Behavior surveyed teens ages 14-17. 63% of 14-year-old boys reported that they had masturbated at least once and 80% of 17-year-old boys reported the same. 43% of 14-year-old girls and 58% of 17-year-old girls reported masturbating at least once.[3] These stats show us that masturbation is very common among teenage boys and girls and we need not shame it or villainize it. It also shows that even if you're in the 20% of 17-year-old boys or 42% of 17-year-old girls who have never masturbated, that's still a *huge* amount of people. There's nothing weird or wrong with you if you've never masturbated.

For parents and pastors reading these stats, we need to understand that the discovery of masturbation is the norm for the majority of male and female teens. We have the responsibility to give needed navigation on this sensitive topic, not shame kids like they've committed the worst sin in the world, when clearly that's not even close to what masturbation is. Most Christian teens are simply stumbling upon masturbation and are looking for some realistic navigation on what to do with something that can lead to worse things or remain pretty neutral.

I don't think we should ever judge or shame the discovery of masturbation. But once it's been discovered, we need to be talking about ways it can be harmful so that it can be navigated in a wise and healthy way (while still not judging and shaming!).

As already explained at length in this book, lust and objectification are not God's design and are harmful to us and others. If thoughts of objectification are accompanying masturbation, we are training our minds to view humans as objects. This is a pattern we need to reject and resist.

We need to be honest about how easily masturbation can lead us to lust and objectifying thoughts. When it does, we are in sin and need to repent and get accountability for this. Be brutally honest with yourself and your inner circle on this one.

Masturbation can also become very addicting and it can become a coping mechanism for stress, boredom, or emotional pain. We need to be aware of this and be intentional about finding healing from pain in healthy places like a counselor's office, our walks with Jesus, and confiding in a trusted friend or youth pastor. Numbing pain with masturbation will prevent us from dealing with our pain in a healthy way. This will only lead to more damaging addictive behaviors as numbing becomes our solution to life's problems.

If you're masturbating daily or multiple times a day, that's a good sign that you need to reach out for some help in breaking the habit, even if this masturbation isn't associated with lustful thoughts.

There's no magic solution to eliminating masturbation from your life and everyone's experience is going to be different. For some, they can simply choose to stop and they are able to. Praise God if this is you.

For many, you'll be able to stop or severely limit how often you masturbate once you stop looking at porn. We've previously talked about how every time you look at porn, you've thrown a new log onto the fire that sends the blaze higher and higher. But your desire for porn will dwindle once you're able to stop throwing on new logs. The same is true for masturbation. The higher those flames are, the more you're going to want to masturbate. You'll masturbate while looking at porn, but the pornographic images will come to mind at any time of day, creating the desire to masturbate even when porn isn't physically present. As you break your porn habit (which I hope the steps in this book will help you do), your desire to masturbate will lessen over time. You won't be adding logs to the fire all the time and the memory of those images will eventually begin to fade, lessening the amount of triggers that spark your desire to masturbate.

The other thing you'll find is that masturbation breeds more masturbation. Your body and mind get used to do doing it. Like I mentioned above, it becomes your way of solving an emotional issue or it simply becomes a ritual. You might start masturbating in the shower, and then every time you take a shower, you want to masturbate. While this trend is discouraging, the encouraging part is that masturbating less breeds less masturbation. Once you start breaking these cycles, rituals, and habits, your mind and body's desire for masturbation will decrease. You get accustomed to not needing it and the urges will lessen.

I'm not encouraging you to masturbate. I'm also not naïve enough to think it isn't already happening a lot and so 1.) We need to lessen the shame around it and actually talk about it, and 2.) We need to stop treating it like it's the same thing as looking at pornography. It's not.

At this, I know some parents or pastors might say, "A sin is a sin," and to some degree that's true. Any single sin separates us from God (Romans 3:23). The tricky thing about masturbation is sometimes it's definitely a sin, sometimes it's not a sin, and other times it easily leads into sin. In my humble opinion, it requires navigation, not a one-size-fits-all prohibition, particularly for adolescents.

Another truth to keep in mind is that while a sin is a sin, not all sin does the same damage. And if we are on a growth journey of sinning less and doing less damaging sins, this needs to be celebrated.

So how does this apply to masturbation? I want to be as biblical as possible, while also being realistic about the consequences of different sins:

Not masturbating is probably the ideal route to shoot for.

Masturbating without thinking lustful or objectifying thoughts is the next best route (and not a sin according to what the Bible tells us). This is *better* than masturbating while thinking lustful or objectifying thoughts.

But masturbating while thinking lustful thoughts is *better* than masturbating while looking at porn. So if you are in the habit of looking at porn while masturbating and you are able to get to the point where you no longer look at porn, but you still masturbate while thinking lustful thoughts, praise God! This is a huge victory.

I had a married guy friend who confessed to me that he had recently masturbated. He was *crushed* by what he had done. To him, it was the exact same thing as if he had had sex with another woman. I'm not saying it's great that he masturbated, but let me be clear: a husband masturbating is nowhere close to being as bad as if he had sex with a woman who wasn't his wife! And to treat the two as the same is to heap an incredibly unnecessary pile of shame onto ourselves, and it doesn't allow us to celebrate the victories over sin that we do experience. I know none of you are married so the illustration isn't an exact fit, but I hope you can see the point I'm trying to make as it relates to the "better than" steps of masturbation that I outlined above.

The path to getting out of a porn / lust / objectification addiction is very long and winding. We must celebrate all of the steps of victory along the way, not just the point far off in the future when we reach perfection (as if that were even possible!). If you are looking at porn while masturbating, and you are able to stop porn and only masturbate, celebrate that! If you are masturbating and lusting, and you are able to masturbate without lusting, celebrate that! If you are able to masturbate less frequently, celebrate that! Keep that trajectory up and see how strong you are able to get.

Part of my fear in writing this section on masturbation is that I know there are a lot of different views on it and I'm afraid you will throw out the rest of the book if you disagree with anything I've written here. This is especially true if you are a parent or pastor previewing this before giving it to your teens. Please don't throw out what I feel is life-saving content in the rest of this book because we may disagree on this final point. I write it with humility and want you to know it's not a hill I want to die on. I just believe it's better to stumble through an attempt at navigation on a gray area like one than give a blanket prohibition or not talk about it at all, both of which leave teens in the dark when it comes to figuring all of this out in real time. The dark is where things always spiral out of control. If nothing else, I hope I've started some conversations in trusted inner circles about masturbation and I pray the Holy Spirit will lead and guide all involved.

CONCLUSION

You can achieve incredible victory over the addictive traps of porn and sex and lust in your life, but there will always be new and deeper temptation to meet you next. "Deeper" in the sense that it isn't surface level. They will be about strengthening your heart and your mind. There are deeper levels of maturity in how you view all men and women. How you sacrificially love your spouse if you get married. God never tires of shaping our hearts to be more and more like his. So when we take any step on the journey away from a more destructive habit and toward a less destructive and more life-giving pattern, we must celebrate that.

Speaking of something to genuinely celebrate, you've made it to the end of this book! As I said in the introduction, reading this book takes incredible courage and you did it. I celebrate you and all that God is doing in your life. I now challenge you to read the book again with a friend or group of friends. If you already read it with some friends, reach out to some new friends and read it with them. One of the best ways to find freedom from these sins is to be used by God to help others find freedom from these sins. Now go…and be used by God! He is longing to use you, and you will find no better purpose or meaning in life than this.

You are our Father's son or daughter, and he loves you so much. He is so pleased with you. Nothing can add or subtract to how much he loves you and approves of you right now.

SMALL GROUP DISCUSSION QUESTIONS

CHAPTER 6

1. What were your biggest takeaways from this book?

2. What action steps are you taking as a result of reading this book?

3. How is God inviting you to see his love for you differently and more deeply? Brainstorm with your group some ways you can be reminded of this love on a regular basis.

4. Who do you need to continue to be in conversation and community with regarding being free from porn and sexual sin? This should be a person or people who you can pray with, remind each other of truths, and hold each other accountable.

FURTHER RESOURCES

On LGBTQ+ / Same Sex Attraction - *Living in a Gray World: A Christian Teen's Guide to Understanding Homosexuality* by Preston Sprinkle (Grand Rapids, MI: Zondervan, 2015)

The Center for Faith, Sexuality & Gender
   www.centerforfaith.com

On masturbation - "Is Masturbation a Sin?" blog article by Noah Filipiak www.noahfilipiak.com/is-masturbation-a-sin

For guys – *Beyond the Battle: A man's guide to his identity in Christ in an oversexualized world* by Noah Filipiak (Grand Rapids, MI: Zondervan, 2021)

For ladies – *90 Days to Wholeness: A porn addiction recovery devotional and coloring journal for women* (Updated paperback edition) by Crystal Renaud Day (Kansas City: Living on Purpose, 2020)

SheRecovery Teen Girls Recovery Group –
www.sherecovery.com/sherecovery-teens-virtual-meetings/

NOTES

ABOUT THIS BOOK

1. Noah Filipiak, *Beyond the Battle: A Man's Guide to His Identity in Christ in an Oversexualized World* (Grand Rapids, MI: Zondervan, 2021)
2. https://scholars.unh.edu/cgi/viewcontent.cgi?article=1283&context=soc_facpub
3. https://www.researchgate.net/publication/221980235_Pornography_Use_Who_Uses_It_and_How_It_Is_Associated_with_Couple_Outcomes
4. Solano, I., Eaton, N. R., & O'Leary, K. D. (2020). Pornography Consumption, Modality and Function in a Large Internet Sample. Journal of sex research, 57(1), 92–103. https://doi.org/10.1080/00224499.2018.1532488
5. Preston Sprinkle, *Living in a Gray World: A Christian Teen's Guide to Understanding Homosexuality* (Grand Rapids, MI: Zondervan, 2015)

2. WHAT'S THE PROBLEM WITH PORN?

1. 1. Robb, M.B., & Mann, S. (2023). Teens and pornography. San Francisco, CA: Common Sense.
2. Number of reported forcible rape cases in the United States from 1990 to 2022. Published by Statista Research Department, Oct 20, 2023. https://www.statista.com/statistics/191137/reported-forcible-rape-cases-in-the-usa-since-1990/
3. Robb, M.B., & Mann, S. (2023). Teens and pornography. San Francisco, CA: Common Sense.
4. https://www.covenanteyes.com/pornstats/
5. Manning J., Senate Testimony 2004, referencing: Dedmon, J., "Is the internet bad for your marriage? Online affairs, pornographic sites playing greater role in divorces," 2002, press release from The Dilenschneider Group, Inc.
6. www.beyondthebattle.net – If you're a guy age 18+, join us!
7. Maddox, A. M., Rhoades, G. K., & Markman, H. J. (2011). Viewing Sexually-Explicit Materials Alone Or Together: Associations With

Relationship Quality. Archives Of Sexual Behavior, 40(2), 441-448. Doi:10.1007/S10508-009-9585-4

8. Harper, C., & Hodgins, D. C. (2016). Examining Correlates of Problematic internet Pornography Use Among University Students. Journal of behavioral addictions, 5(2), 179–191. https://doi.org/10.1556/2006.5.2016.022

9. Wordecha, M., Wilk, M., Kowalewska, E., Skorko, M., Łapiński, A., & Gola, M. (2018). 'Pornographic binges' as a key characteristic of males seeking treatment for compulsive sexual behaviors: Qualitative and quantitative 10-week-long diary assessment. Journal of behavioral addictions, 7(2), 433–444. https://doi.org/10.1556/2006.7.2018.33

10. Butler, M. H., Pereyra, S. A., Draper, T. W., Leonhardt, N. D., & Skinner, K. B. (2018). Pornography Use and Loneliness: A Bidirectional Recursive Model and Pilot Investigation. Journal of sex & marital therapy, 44(2), 127–137. https://doi.org/10.1080/0092623X.2017.1321601

11. Willoughby, B. J., Young-Petersen, B., & Leonhardt, N. D. (2018). Exploring trajectories of pornography use through adolescence and emerging adulthood.55(3), 297-309. doi:10.1080/00224499.2017.1368977

12. Koletić G. (2017). Longitudinal associations between the use of sexually explicit material and adolescents' attitudes and behaviors: A narrative review of studies. Journal of adolescence, 57, 119–133. https://doi.org/10.1016/j.adolescence.2017.04.006

13. Patrick Carnes, *Out of the Shadows,* Third Edition (Center City, MN: Hazelden, 2001), 30.

14. Banca, P., Morris, L. S., Mitchell, S., Harrison, N. A., Potenza, M. N., & Voon, V. (2016). Novelty, conditioning and attentional bias to sexual rewards. Journal of psychiatric research, 72, 91–101. doi: 10.1016/j.jpsychires.2015.10.017

15. Kuhn, S., & Gallinat, J. (2014). Brain Structure and Functional Connectivity Associated With Pornography Consumption: The Brain on Porn. JAMA Psychiatry, 71(7), 827-834. doi:10.1001/jamapsychiatry.2014.93

16. British Board of Film Classification. (2020). Young people, pornography & age-verification. BBFC. Retrieved from https://www.bbfc.co.uk/about-classification/research

17. Martellozzo, E., Monaghan, A., Adler, J. R., Davidson, J., Leyva, R., & Horvath, M. A. H. (2016). 'I wasn't sure it was normal to watch it'. London: NSPCC. Retrieved from https://learning.nspcc.org.uk/research-resources/2016/i-wasn-t-sure-it-was-normal-to-watch-it

18. Fritz, N., Malic, V., Paul, B., & Zhou, Y. (2020). A descriptive analysis of the types, targets, and relative frequency of aggression in main-

stream pornography. Archives of Sexual Behavior, 49(8), 3041-3053. doi:10.1007/s10508-020-01773-0

19. Bridges, A. J., Wosnitzer, R., Scharrer, E., Sun, C. & Liberman, R. (2010). Aggression and Sexual Behavior in Best Selling Pornography Videos: A Content Analysis Update. Violence Against Women, 16(10), 1065–1085. doi:10.1177/1077801210382866

20. Bridges, A. J., Wosnitzer, R., Scharrer, E., Sun, C. & Liberman, R. (2010). Aggression and Sexual Behavior in Best Selling Pornography Videos: A Content Analysis Update. Violence Against Women, 16(10), 1065–1085. doi:10.1177/1077801210382866

21. Martellozzo, E., Monaghan, A., Adler, J. R., Davidson, J., Leyva, R., & Horvath, M. A. H. (2016). 'I wasn't sure it was normal to watch it'. London: NSPCC. Retrieved from https://learning.nspcc.org.uk/research-resources/2016/i-wasn-t-sure-it-was-normal-to-watch-it

22. https://www.cdc.gov/violenceprevention/sexualviolence/fastfact.html

23. United States Department of Health and Human Services, "Human Trafficking Fact Sheet" (2004), https://www.hsdl.org/?view&did=23329.

24. *Global Estimates of Modern Slavery: Forced Labour and Forced Marriage* (Geneva: International Labour Organization, 2017), 39–40, https://www.ilo.org/wcmsp5/groups/public/---dgreports/---dcomm/documents/publication/wcms_575479.pdf.

25. Development Services Group, Inc., "Commercial Sexual Exploitation of Children Sex Trafficking: Literature Review," Office of Juvenile Justice and Delinquency Prevention (2014), 2, https://ojjdp.ojp.gov/mpg/literature-review/csec-sex-trafficking.pdf.

26. United States Department of Justice, National Center for Missing and Exploited Children, Demi and Ashton Foundation, cited in web page sidebar for Youth Radio, "Trafficked Teen Girls Describe Life in 'The Game,' " *All Things Considered*, December 6, 2010, https://www.npr.org/2010/12/06/131757019/youth-radio-trafficked-teen-girls-describe-life-in-the-game.

27. Noah Filipiak, *Beyond the Battle* (Grand Rapids, MI: Zondervan, 2021), 88-89.

28. McKenna, Chris (2020). Porn and ED: 3 Peer-Reviewed Studies You Need to Read. https://www.covenanteyes.com/2017/08/09/does-science-support-pied-part-2/

4. FILLING THAT EMPTINESS

1. Jim Wilder and Michel Hendricks describe how showing this type of love to another physically changes and heals our brains (*The Other Half of Church: Christian Community, Brain Science, and Overcoming Spiritual Stagnation* [Chicago: Moody, 2020], 79-90).
2. www.beyondthebattle.net – If you're a guy age 18+, join us!

5. HOW TO STOP LOOKING AT PORN

1. Sederer, Lloyd, MD (2019). What Does "Rat Park" Teach Us About Addiction? https://www.psychiatrictimes.com/view/what-does-rat-park-teach-us-about-addiction

6. NAVIGATING PURITY CULTURE

1. Joshua Harris, *I Kissed Dating Goodbye: A New Attitude Toward Romance and Relationships* (Colorado Springs, CO: Multnomah Books, 1997)
2. Hopkins, M.K. (1965). "The age of Roman girls at marriage". *Population Studies*. **18** (3): 309–327.
3. Robbins, C., Schick, V., Reece, M. (2011). 'Prevalence, Frequency, and Associations of Masturbation With Partnered Sexual Behaviors Among US Adolescents.' National Survey of Sexual Health and Behavior. https://jamanetwork.com/journals/jamapediatrics/fullarticle/1107656?resultClick=1

Made in the USA
Columbia, SC
24 September 2024